Stop Smoking

Strategies For Overcoming Nicotine Dependence And
Achieving Optimal Health Without Weight Gain

*(The Key To Cessation Of Alcohol Consumption And
Tobacco Addiction)*

Gerard Brisebois

TABLE OF CONTENT

The Genesis Of My Nicotine Dependency 1

Strategies For Harnessing The Power Of The Law Of Attraction 9

Effects Of Quitting Smoking 21

What Is The Optimal Approach To Cessation Of Smoking? 65

The Effects Of Smoking 87

The Negative Ramifications Of Smoking 103

Daily Habits For Assisting Smoking Cessation 128

The Genesis Of My Nicotine Dependency

Engaging in tobacco consumption greatly increases the risk of a protracted demise. I am Angelo, and I initiated the habit of smoking at the age of seventeen. Paradoxically, it never occurred to me that I possessed the inclination to partake in smoking a cigarette. The act of smoking by my mother was something I strongly despised, prompting me to form a solemn commitment to abstain from ever engaging in such a detrimental habit, let alone partake in smoking itself. The actions of others did not have any impact or sway on my own personal stance or decision. I have consistently exhibited independent thinking and have never been prone to following others. Furthermore, I was well aware that my mother would strongly disapprove if she were to discover any tendencies I had towards negative habits.

My acquaintances engaged in the act of smoking in close proximity to my person and frequently extended the courtesy of offering me a tobacco product. Mani, one of my acquaintances, adamantly refused to accept a negative response. He exemplified the characteristics commonly associated with individuals of Hispanic heritage. Have I already discussed the fact that my upbringing took place in Central America? Yes, I did, precisely in Panama. It remains unclear as to why individuals of Hispanic origin often exhibit assertive behavior. We are determined to find a positive outcome despite encountering rejection. Undoubtedly, my friend Mani comprehended the situation and ceased presenting me with cigarettes subsequent to my resolute expression of disapproval towards smoking. Furthermore, being an adolescent without employment, my mother did not tolerate such behavior.

On the third of November in the year 1997, my acquaintances and I were commemorating the national holiday that represents the liberation of our nation. In Panama, we observe Independence Day in a manner that differs slightly from the practices observed in the United States. It is a festive celebration in which all the educational institutions partake in a collective parade through the central city of Panama. The entire nation, comprising of the president and the first lady, gathers to witness and partake in the enchanting celebrations throughout the course of the day. It is truly splendid to take part in. Everyone drinks beer, has a good time, and dance in the streets to salsa, soca, tipico, and all types of latino vibes. On this particular evening, Mani, who was of Hispanic descent, displayed a tendency towards generosity by offering me a cigarette, which I accepted and subsequently smoked. I pondered inwardly, "What is the significance of this matter?" It's just one'. Mani directed his gaze towards me, conveying approval through a nod while simultaneously offering me a cigarette, which he proceeded to ignite. During the period in which I engaged in the consumption of tobacco and alcoholic beverages, I discerned a distinct alteration in my emotional state. It produced a distinct sensation, offering me a sense of relaxation and tranquility. Subsequently, I found myself progressively increasing my tobacco consumption. On each occasion that I consumed a beverage, I was also engaging in the act of smoking a carcinogenic substance. The term my spouse used to refer to cigarettes was incredibly vexing to me when I heard her utter it. I consistently engaged in smoking and, over time, it evolved into an addictive habit deeply ingrained in my lifestyle.

By this point, I had established a daily smoking habit, but I took measures to ensure that I was distanced from my place of residence. I had no desire for my mother to become aware of my smoking habit. She was completely oblivious...... little did I know! I concealed the cigarettes in my drawer, unaware of my mother's regular inspections during my absence. Therefore, she discovered my cigarettes but chose not to inform me. I believed that I had successfully evaded consequences! To my surprise, one day she approached me with a request to acquire one of my cigarettes. I experienced a confluence of emotions, namely astonishment, apprehension, fear, and humiliation, simultaneously. I lowered my head and confessed, "I...I...do not engage in smoking, Mother!" To this, she retorted, "Indeed? Then kindly elucidate as to why I discovered cigarettes within your dresser drawer." To whom does it belong?"

I eventually came to the realization that I could no longer deceive my mother. It was in my utmost advantage to honestly divulge the information and disclose the truth to my mother. So I did. Her level of anger was not as intense as I had expected. It is my conjecture that she perceived it as incongruous to express anger towards me while engaging in the identical behavior. As an alternative, she proposed engaging in a deliberation on the matter, which proved thought-provoking yet anxiety-inducing. She had a desire to ascertain the identities, details, timing, locations, and reasons behind the matter. I disclosed all pertinent information to her, and in response, she responded with a smile and embraced me, assuring me of her unwavering love regardless of the circumstances. I experienced a sense of alleviation as I held disdain towards causing her dissatisfaction. Subsequently, I continued the habit of smoking for a duration of seventeen years. As my smoking escalated, the deterioration of my physical health became increasingly pronounced. I perceived its presence on a daily basis. I commenced the act of consecutive smoking (engaging in the consumption of multiple cigarettes without interruption). I experienced a deterioration of my nervous state and as a result, experienced pronounced tremors. In addition to my breath, it was remarkably unpleasant. Frankly, I am still perplexed by my wife's ability to withstand such challenging circumstances for all those years. Tobacco consumption is a substance dependency, and I was a person suffering from substance abuse. It is permissible by law to attain such an elevated state. My physical reliance on it was so profound that there were moments when I doubted my ability to ever abandon it. Certain aspects of myself were reluctant to cease my endeavors. It had become an integral facet of my existence.

Strategies For Harnessing The Power Of The Law Of Attraction

The principle underlying the law of attraction centers around the notion that any occurrence, be it favorable or unfavorable, transpires due to one's own active magnetic pull towards it. Even in the absence of deliberate enforcement of the law, events still transpire as a result of our inherent propensity to draw them towards ourselves. If you're broke and a friend gave you some money or loaned you or gave you a job, it happened because at some point you thought about that and you attracted it to you. If your day commenced with a negative atmosphere, it is likely due to your own attraction of such circumstances. Indeed, the principle of attraction operates incessantly in our daily lives, regardless of our level of conscious recognition. If one holds the belief and conviction that an event or outcome will come to fruition, it is highly likely that it shall indeed transpire.

Thus, what measures can we implement to leverage this principle? Proceed by adhering to these straightforward yet impactful guidelines:

1. Engage in meditation: Enhance your cognitive abilities by devoting a minimum of 10 minutes of your schedule to the practice of meditation. This activity promotes mental relaxation and enhances cognitive abilities. This is strongly advised, although not compulsory.

2. Ensure that you possess a clear understanding of your desires and eliminate any traces of uncertainty. If you wish to attain something, ensure that your level of determination is sufficiently high to attract its manifestation from the universe. This indicates that your desired outcome must be definite, and you should possess a strong level of certainty about it. Eliminate any trace of uncertainty, for it shall inevitably permeate your thoughts and hinder the universe from bringing

about your desires precisely as envisioned.

3. Envision: It is not uncommon to hear individuals of great accomplishment express sentiments such as "What was once an abstract concept in my mind has now become my reality" or "My aspirations have transformed into tangible achievements." This implies that in order to accomplish something, it is crucial to envision oneself experiencing that desired outcome. As an illustration, suppose your aspiration is to become a top-level executive. Envision yourself occupying an executive chair within an expansive and luxurious office, situated within a renowned corporation that you have successfully founded. Ensure that your visualization is articulated with precision, such that the cosmos may perceive your authentic aspirations and bestow them upon you. If you possess profound infatuation towards an individual, endeavor to conceive and actively portray a scenario in which you are in the company of said person. When

your longing intensifies and you relentlessly strive for this outcome, it is within the realm of possibility for the universe to bestow it upon you.

4. Transcribing and experiencing it: Engaging in the act of creating a comprehensive compilation of the desires you possess instigates a sharpened concentration upon those aspects that hold utmost significance to you. It is more conducive to the process of visualization and cognitive engagement to physically transcribe and represent one's thoughts and ideas on paper. Do not hesitate to record your desire. Perceive the unfolding of events and respond as if they have already transpired, as if they are currently unfolding in your immediate presence. Do not be negative. Believe that it's happening. The essence of the application of the law of attraction lies primarily in one's emotional state. When one's cognitive processes are influenced by their emotional state, the pace of decision-making tends to be expedited.

5. Expressing gratitude enables the smooth manifestation of the law of attraction. Learn to express gratitude for all the blessings bestowed upon you. Express gratitude to the cosmos for all the occurrences and experiences that have befallen upon you. Even simple things count. Expressing gratitude elicits a positive reflection. It has been observed that expressing gratitude towards an individual for their generosity or actions prompts a heightened likelihood of future additional contributions or acts of kindness from said individual, as well as a heightened sense of satisfaction on their part. It is likewise applicable to the cosmos. Expressing gratitude is indicative of a positive mindset, thereby fostering an environment that draws positive outcomes.

6. Have faith and confidence: If you desire something, release it; if it returns to you, it is destined for you, if it does not, it was never meant to be. This implies that when aspiring for a certain goal, it is essential to have faith and

confidence in the Universe's ability to bestow it upon you. Don't wait for it. Have faith in its occurrence and refrain from excessive dependency. In the event that it does not occur promptly, refrain from becoming displeased. There exists an allocated period for every action. Your opportunity will duly present itself in due course and under appropriate circumstances. When one maintains belief and confidence, the envisioned outcome is more likely to manifest itself as reality.

INTRODUCTION TO SMOKING

The year was 1997 when I was in my third year of high school. I began occasionally indulging in a few drags here and there, and from that point on, I found myself ensnared in the perilous realm of cigarette smoking. During that period, many of my classmates engaged in smoking, while we indulged in exuberant partying. Apart from our smoking habit, we also partook in heavy drinking on weekends. Hence, it can be inferred that alcohol consumption and smoking went hand in hand for us. I consumed an entire pack of cigarettes daily, which is suboptimal for an individual of slender build such as myself, and it certainly did not align with a healthy lifestyle.

I made the choice to persist in the habit of smoking, and I was greeted enthusiastically by the younger generation. I experienced a heightened sense of competence while engaging in the consumption of tobacco and alcohol. Each moment spent smoking a cigarette was a source of immense pleasure, and I derived great enjoyment from the experience.

Upon discovering this, my parents became aware, and I anticipated receiving a barrage of discourse regarding the detrimental consequences of smoking. Nevertheless, I persisted in my actions. I refrained from smoking in their presence, which necessitates me concealing my smoking activities whenever I am indoors.

On a regular basis, I engaged in smoking during the morning hours prior to attending school, and subsequently consumed a significant amount of cigarettes in the aftermath of my classes. To put it mildly, I developed a profound affinity for smoking—I found great pleasure in it. After each meal, during periods of boredom, and during social interactions, I would consistently engage in smoking. Gradually, the habit of smoking began to consume a significant portion of my time and focus, and the notion of quitting had not even crossed my mind.

Two years post-graduation, my comrades from high school entered into a collective agreement to refrain from tobacco use and, as a result, I successfully left behind that habit. The sense of elation that ensued was truly remarkable.

Several years have elapsed, and I believed I had escaped, yet it appears to have eluded me thus far. For a duration of four years, I abstained from smoking. Subsequently, I resumed smoking and continued the habit for a period of twenty years. Frequently, I have experienced the desire to engage in smoking.

The habit of smoking has peculiar methods of infiltrating both your mind and body. It has garnered widespread recognition as the most enslaving indulgence, surpassing both coffee, alcoholic beverages, and certain forms of narcotics.

So there it was, she was back into my system. The addiction reemerged, surpassing its previous state, as I indulged in significantly greater amounts of smoking. She was omnipresent, in every place, at all times. Upon arising each morning, subsequent to meals, during designated lunch intervals, whilst commuting by vehicle, preceding the act of bathing, whilst consuming beverages. She exhibited a higher degree of malevolence, swiftness, and prowess. It appears that I have exhausted my efforts in finding a way to have her depart from my presence.

I strategically chose to persist with smoking. Nevertheless, I recognized the need to counteract its effects by consuming nourishing foods and engaging in regular physical activity, and thus proceeded accordingly. It did not significantly perturb me; I was cognizant that should I persist on this trajectory, I would need to mitigate the adverse impact of smoking. I endeavored to conduct thorough research on the types of foods and vitamins that mitigate the consequences of smoking. Additionally, I exerted utmost discipline to limit my daily cigarette intake to precisely one pack.

Over the passage of time, I have failed to observe any adverse consequences arising from the act of smoking.

Furthermore, I have come to recognize that it enhances my cognitive abilities, accelerates my mental processing, and potentially fortifies my physical capabilities. I became heavily addicted to smoking and coffee, and the combination of both substances had an astonishing impact on me. I experienced enhanced cognitive capabilities, leading to improved decision-making and efficiency. By synergistically combining caffeine and nicotine, I perceived a notable increase in productivity, resulting in significantly smoother outcomes.

The majority of individuals who smoke have most likely experienced this comparable situation. From a practical standpoint, it has historically proven to be a less secure and conducive path to follow. The majority of individuals ensnared by the grip of this addiction, who are amongst the smoking populace, have experienced profound remorse for initiating their journey into smoking. It is essential to bear in mind the origin of the addiction—the point of its inception. In this manner, you can ascertain a method to extricate yourself and effect the necessary adaptations.

Take a moment to reflect on when you commenced the habit of smoking. By adopting such an approach, you are able to determine the underlying source of the issue.

Effects Of Quitting Smoking

The Physiological Effects of Smoking Cessation on the Human Body

The aforementioned advantages of ceasing cigarette consumption are comprehensive, nevertheless, it is intriguing to conduct a systematic examination of the physiological changes that occur in a smoker's body upon quitting smoking.

In order to provide a more comprehensive understanding of the benefits one can expect upon ceasing the habit of smoking, we will now examine the immediate as well as long-term implications that result from quitting smoking.

Shortly after you abstain from smoking for 20 minutes, your body initiates a series of transformations that serve as the cornerstone for all subsequent advantages. The heart rate gradually slows down, reaching levels that are considered within the normal range. This is accompanied by a decrease in heart rate as well.

As the duration of abstaining from smoking exceeds two hours, the alterations experienced manifest even more noticeably. The heart rate and blood pressure will gradually approach levels within the range considered as normal. Moreover, there will be an improvement in circulation, leading to increased blood flow to the extremities. Anticipate a sensation of increased warmth in your toes and fingers. Nevertheless, nicotine withdrawal symptoms will manifest, yielding intense cravings, heightened anxiety, elevated appetite, insomnia, and various other associated challenges. These symptoms merely represent the initial manifestations of withdrawal.

After the passage of twelve hours without smoking, the oxygen levels in your bloodstream undergo a restorative process. The act of smoking cigarettes results in the generation of carbon monoxide. It is imperative to acknowledge that carbon monoxide forms bonds with blood cells more readily when compared to oxygen. Elevated levels of carbon monoxide can pose a health hazard to the human body. After abstaining from smoking for a period of twelve hours, the presence of carbon monoxide in the bloodstream gradually diminishes while the amount of oxygen being carried by it increases. This signifies the restoration of the levels to their standard condition.

One of the significant health consequences associated with the act of smoking tobacco is the elevated likelihood of experiencing a myocardial infarction. Individuals who engage in smoking tobacco products typically experience an elevated risk, approximately 70% higher, of suffering from heart attacks in comparison to those who do not partake in smoking.

Nevertheless, it is imperative to acknowledge that this constitutes one of the reversible consequences of smoking. Once you have refrained from smoking for a full day, your circulatory system begins its journey towards recuperation, gradually reducing the ongoing likelihood of a heart attack.

The resilience of the human body is astounding as it effortlessly embarks on the process of regeneration, despite enduring years of deterioration resulting from the consumption of tobacco through smoking. Individuals who engage in the act of smoking tend to experience a diminished sense of smell and taste in general. This sensation of numbness is often inconspicuous, owing to its gradual onset. Nevertheless, within a mere two-day timeframe following the cessation of smoking, a discernible enhancement in the senses of taste and smell can be observed. The injured nerve endings initiate a gradual process of regeneration, thereby reviving functionality in your taste receptors.

After a period of three days, the advantages of ceasing smoking are consistently manifesting themselves, although the accompanying symptoms of withdrawal are equally persistent. By this juncture, the nicotine shall have dissipated from your system. As your body had already become accustomed to metabolizing nicotine, its absence presents a formidable challenge. At this juncture, appetitive yearnings will reach their pinnacle, and individuals may begin experiencing corporeal unease characterized by headaches and nausea. This is typically a challenging period, and it is advisable to have an effective mechanism for managing it. Make an effort to redirect your attention towards finding enjoyment in other activities. This is an opportune moment to treat yourself amidst the challenges you are facing, albeit refraining from indulging in tobacco.

After a few weeks, the fruits of your efforts are beginning to amass. Your physical wellbeing will have experienced a substantial improvement, with a notable decrease in withdrawal symptoms and likely reaching their minimum level, resulting in an enhanced overall state of being. Your respiratory system will experience significant improvement, resulting in enhanced lung clarity and greatly improved circulation. You can perform physically strenuous activities, such as running, without experiencing respiratory difficulty.

The body's regenerative process persists and results in noteworthy benefits after approximately nine months. Firstly, the withdrawal symptoms will have subsided and ceased entirely. Your pulmonary system, which serves as the epicenter for the repercussions of smoking, will have commenced the process of restoration. The consumption of tobacco has the detrimental effect of impairing the normal functioning of the cilia. Cilia refer to the diminutive filamentous structures situated along the inner lining of the trachea, which effectively facilitate the movement of mucus outwards from the respiratory organs. They aid in minimizing the probability of contracting an infection. They undergo a process of regeneration and gradually restore complete functionality within a few months of discontinuing cigarette smoking, thereby mitigating the typical susceptibility to infections associated with smokers. You are now able to avail a reduced number of sick leave.

After the completion of a year, there will be numerous accomplishments to commemorate. Throughout the entirety of the cardiac recovery process, and following one year of abstinence from smoking, an individual will be eligible to assert a decreased likelihood of experiencing a heart attack. To specify, at present, the likelihood of experiencing a heart attack is reduced by 50% in comparison to individuals who continue to smoke.

Engaging in the act of smoking is closely linked to the constriction of blood vessels, subsequently giving rise to an increased susceptibility to the occurrence of stroke. This is particularly evident due to the heightened presence of carbon monoxide, alongside various other toxic substances found in cigarettes. Following a period of five to fifteen years, the blood vessels will have undergone an extensive restoration process, returning to their optimal dimensions and thereby diminishing the likelihood of stroke to that comparable to an individual without any predisposition.

One of the primary hazards associated with smoking is the potential to develop a range of cancers, specifically including lung cancer. It is noteworthy to observe that in the absence of smoking, lung cancer would be an infrequent manifestation of the disease. Smokers account for over 90% of lung cancer cases. After a decade, the probability of developing lung cancer is reduced by

50% in comparison to that experienced by habitual smokers. The incidence of additional malignancies, such as cancer of the throat, mouth, and stomach resulting from smoking, also decreases.

The milestone of fifteen years is of utmost importance in terms of diminishing the likelihood of developing any cardiovascular ailments. The likelihood of experiencing anginas, arrhythmias, coronary diseases, and heart infections will considerably diminish, resulting in an improved state of health. At this juncture, individuals who have successfully ceased smoking will possess an equivalent propensity for experiencing a heart attack as individuals who have never engaged in smoking.

Based on the results of conducted research, it has been determined that individuals who do not smoke tend to have a lifespan that exceeds that of individuals who engage in smoking habits by approximately fifteen years.

This implies that for every year you abstain from smoking, you are increasing your lifespan. Former individuals who have successfully ceased their smoking habit prior to reaching the age of thirty five are believed to potentially prolong their lifespans by approximately five to ten years, whereas those in the age bracket of sixty and above may experience an extension of about three years in their life expectancy. This proves that, there is always something to look forward to when you decide to quit and that decision can be taken at any point in life. This represents the enduring advantage of ceasing the habit of cigarette smoking.

Chapter 3:
Hourly Basis
Synopsis

This concept is imparted by nearly all platforms dedicated to addressing substance abuse or any form of emotional struggle. The frequent citation of this statement can be attributed to its extensive relevance to nearly all distressing circumstances. Approach each day as it unfolds.

Accept things as they occur" or "Embrace events as they transpire

Addressing the issue of smoking cessation is equally applicable. In addition to refraining from picking up another cigarette, adopting a mindset that embraces the present moment, whether it be on a daily or hourly basis, serves as the primary strategy that empowers smokers to effectively cease smoking and break free from the overwhelming clutches of nicotine addiction.

When initially abstaining from smoking, adopting the mindset of approaching each day or each hour as it unfolds proves to be markedly advantageous, as opposed to the smoker entertaining the belief of permanent abstinence.

On this occasion, the smoker is initiating the act of quitting smoking; however, he is uncertain as to whether he desires to live the remainder of his life without smoking. Frequently, smokers perceive life without smoking as more arduous, dreadful, and devoid of amusement.

Only after he stops smoking does he come to understand that his previous notions about life as a non-smoker were incorrect. Upon his resignation, he acknowledges that there is existence beyond tobacco consumption.

It represents a life that is more pristine, tranquil, abundant, and above all, imbued with enhanced well-being. Now the idea of resuming smoking has become an abhorrent notion. Despite the heightened concerns, it is imperative to uphold the approach of embracing each day as it unfolds.

Now, even though he has quit smoking, he still experiences occasional unpleasant moments. Occasionally, as a result of heightened domestic or occupational stress, uncomfortable social environments, or other ambiguous travel circumstances, the inclination to smoke increases. He simply needs to affirm to himself that he will abstain from smoking for the duration of the current day and defer any concerns or thoughts about tomorrow.

The momentary urge will dissipate within a few minutes, and it is probable that he will not even contemplate smoking the next day. Nevertheless, the principle of living in the present should not solely be limited to situations involving a strong desire. It is imperative to engage in daily practice. Occasionally, a former smoker may perceive these thought patterns as no longer imperative.

He acquiesces to the notion that he will abstain from smoking indefinitely. Assuming his correctness, at what point does he commend himself for accomplishing his objective? As he lies on his deathbed, he may fervently declare, "I never indulged in another cigarette." What an opportune moment for a remarkable commendation.

Each day, the former smoker should awaken with the intention of abstaining from smoking throughout the entirety of the day. Before retiring for the night, it is recommended that he commend himself for his unwavering commitment to his objective. Maintaining one's pride is crucial in the pursuit of a smoke-free lifestyle.

It is not merely significant, but also duly deserved. Those individuals who have successfully abstained from smoking have liberated themselves from a formidable and highly compelling dependence. After an extended period, he has finally established dominion over his life, instead of succumbing to the influence of his smoking habits. Therefore, he should take pride in this.

Therefore, when you retire for the night, commend yourself for successfully abstaining from smoking and declare, "I have achieved an additional smoke-free day; I feel highly satisfied." And upon awakening tomorrow, affirm with conviction, "I am determined to embrace another day without smoking." Tomorrow, I shall deliberate upon the events that lie ahead. In order to preserve one's freedom from smoking, it is crucial to approach each day, and even each hour, with adaptability and resolve, ensuring that one never indulges in the act of smoking again.

Could you kindly provide more information about this Program or Process?

I have undertaken the challenge of overcoming my smoking addiction through a structured approach that I frequently refer to as my Program or Process. And you may be seeking clarification regarding the subject matter I am referring to or its significance.

I have extensively examined methodologies for motivation and effective goal setting, delving into areas such as CBT (Cognitive Behavioral Therapy), DBT (Dialectical Behavioral Therapy), as well as various non-smoking programs including 12-step programs. Equipped with this acquired knowledge, I have devised a highly effective template for smoking cessation. I have endeavored to develop a literary work that will assist individuals in systematically navigating the process, engaging in introspection, and ultimately achieving permanent cessation of smoking.

The program I am offering will be extended to encompass your needs and requirements. Make it your own.

It is within your discretion to complete the template with your own motivation and customization, and I will provide assistance throughout the process. This procedure is divided into two separate components. The initial component presents an extensive array of empirical knowledge pertaining to smoking and its resulting repercussions. The latter portion primarily entails utilizing this foundation as a source of motivation, examining additional factors that can contribute to motivation, and commencing the process of abstaining from smoking. Despite the potential lack of excitement in the initial phase, it remains imperative for fostering your recuperation and is seamlessly incorporated within the program. I suggest that you engage in both aspects for optimal outcomes.

You must exhibit unwavering commitment, possess a strong desire to overcome smoking, and invest diligent effort to attain favorable outcomes. If you are unable to perform this task, then this book is not suited for you. There is no easy, no-work, long-term smoking cure, no matter what anyone claims.

Initiate the first step: Acquire a journal.

You will require a journal of some sort for the completion of this program. A higher level of niceness is preferable as it demonstrates dedication, although the use of lined paper that is consistently stored in a designated location is also acceptable. These assignments can also be completed using your personal computer. Please maintain a high level of organization by diligently labeling items and keeping them securely consolidated. In this manner, we can revisit previous assignments for the purpose of reinforcing our knowledge and fostering introspection.

Allow me to extend my hearty congratulations on your acquisition of a journal, which symbolizes a significant leap forward. Although it may appear insignificant, it is essential to recognize that it indeed represents a profound change in your mindset. You may have previously endeavored to cease the act of smoking or any other habitual behavior, and alas, to no avail. We all have. However, you have recently demonstrated an action that conveys your sincere desire to improve your well-being and your intention to give up the habit of smoking. You will need to continue nurturing that motivation and dedication, but you have taken an initial stride towards that, and you should feel a sense of accomplishment.

PART ONE

These assignments are discretionary, yet they are designed to enhance your advantages. The further you delve into the essence of your addiction, the more favorable your outcome will be.

Addiction encompasses both suffering and gratification. The reason behind your addiction primarily stems from the fact that, in the majority of cases, it provides a certain level of gratification or fulfillment. For the initial assignment, I kindly request you to document your present circumstances. The satisfaction derived from the act of smoking, the adverse effects associated with it, your current smoking patterns (such as the number of packs consumed per day), as well as the specific locations and timings of your smoking activities. Describe your habit. In order to commence the process of discontinuing a habit, it is imperative to establish a concise and clear definition of the habit in question.

First Assignment

Please provide an account in your journal detailing your present association with smoking. The good and the bad. Presented herein is a brief exemplification, and you are welcome to provide additional or fewer examples.

My hands tremble whenever I am deprived of my customary cigarettes. I am experiencing an unwelcome reliance on cigarettes. They assist me in obtaining a state of relaxation amidst the demands of a challenging work day. Recently, I visited the nearby store, and to my surprise, the attendant at the counter was well aware of the specific item I intended to purchase. A few packages of cigarettes, sufficient for a few days. He possessed an extensive knowledge of my brand, comprehending its intricacies in their entirety. I experienced considerable embarrassment due to this situation. I find myself susceptible to temptation merely from the sight of a lighter, as it evokes contemplation of the calming act of inhaling smoke. I regret the current situation as it is detrimental to my well-being and appears to be unfavorable among others. I would never want my children to engage in the act of smoking.

Good job. After successfully completing your initial assignment, it is advisable to establish a personal objective to wholeheartedly dedicate yourself, both internally and externally (such as by means of these assignments), to this transformative endeavor. Take a moment to acknowledge and acknowledge the fact that you have accomplished the following: firstly, you have acquired a journal; secondly, you have completed the initial assignment; and most importantly, you have made a commitment to actively participate in the program (the first two accomplishments serve to reinforce the importance of the third).

Smoking Experience Assignment

Please provide a brief summary of your smoking experience using either a concise 1-3 word description or a comprehensive sentence consisting of 5 words. Like this:

Negative, Self-Gratifying, and Consoling

"Confusing" or

I am uncertain as to the rationale behind my obligation.

Alternatively, one could consider engaging in all three activities, as I personally opted to do. The objective is to facilitate introspection pertaining to your addiction and personal encounter. It does not imply that one must perceive it as wholly negative, but rather, being compelled to select a limited number of words to depict the encounter fosters profound introspection. Take your time.

Excellent job! Now, please proceed with the assigned tasks as we transition into the more intricate and monotonous material.

Why quit smoking?

Smoking is associated with numerous detrimental effects, which are too numerous to be comprehensively delineated within this context. I will provide a concise enumeration of the primary reasons, as their recognition and imparting serve a significant purpose in maintaining focus and impelling determination during the cessation process. It emanates an unpleasant odor, negatively impacts one's physical presentation through various means, poses potential risks to one's overall physical well-being, and incurs substantial financial expenses. Moreover, frequently resorting to it implies that one is relying on it as a coping mechanism for actual feelings.

- Changes to the head and face

- Smoking can cause a decrease in oxygen supply, which can have an impact on the ears and lead to mild hearing impairment. The skin is prone to premature wrinkling due to decreased blood circulation caused by smoking, resulting in a dull and ashen complexion. Nicotine constricts a cerebral component, thereby impacting visual function and potentially resulting in diminished nocturnal visual acuity.

- Discolored enamel.

- Cigarettes will cause discoloration to your teeth, resulting in a noticeable yellow hue, as well as potentially staining your nails or fingers.

- Heart

- Tobacco consumption increases your blood pressure, resulting in the exertion of pressure on your heart, potentially leading to its weakening. It elevates the probability of experiencing a cardiac event and developing various illnesses.

- Lungs

- Long-term tobacco use can lead to permanent lung scarring, resulting in a persistent cough. Smoking induces an inflammatory response that may result in dyspnea, among other manifestations.

- Unpleasant oral odor

- The odor of smoke will cling to your breath, as well as your entire physique, including your hair and attire. This can be especially repugnant to individuals who do not smoke. The majority of smokers lack awareness regarding the strong odor emitted by smoke and its persistent presence.

- DNA

- As stated by the smokefree.gov campaign, tobacco consumption (primarily through smoking) is responsible for one-third of all cancer fatalities. Smoking interferes with your genetic material and renders you prone to a wide range of malignancies.

- The condition of diabetes

- Smoking increases the risk of developing diabetes and exacerbates its management challenges.

- The development of a reliance on smoking, resulting in symptoms such as tremors when abstaining from tobacco.

- Impotence • Male sexual dysfunction • Inability to achieve or maintain an erection • Penile erectile insufficiency

Engaging in smoking escalates the likelihood of experiencing erectile dysfunction, which refers to the inability to achieve or sustain an erection. "Cigarette smoke can also inflict harm upon the genetic material in sperm, resulting in potentially detrimental consequences such as infertility or the emergence of genetic abnormalities in offspring" (smokefree.gov).

- Blood and Immune system

- The odour of smoke permeates one's hair, garments, and all other belongings.

- It is exceedingly challenging to remove that odor from your garments and all other surfaces. And even if you are indifferent, others will take notice.

- Monetary expenses associated with tobacco products.

- The price of cigarettes amounts to approximately $8 per pack. The aforementioned pack of sticks commands a significant monetary value, considering the adverse repercussions they are known to induce. And it adds up.

- In the assignment, please calculate the amount of money you allocate towards cigarettes on a weekly or monthly basis. Following that, determine the financial savings you could achieve or the alternative uses for that money.

Assignment on Motivation: Enumerate a minimum of three factors from the aforementioned list that serve as motivations for refraining from smoking. This serves as the initial step towards seeking motivation - acquainting oneself with the empirical justifications for ceasing the habit of smoking. If none of these stimuli arouse or engender your attention, it is imperative to introspect on the underlying reasons and duly record them as well.

For example, one may assert that the impact on one's respiratory system, the adverse social outcomes such as dental discoloration and unpleasant odor, as well as the financial burdens associated with smoking, serve as the driving factors at present.

Excellent job! You persist in diligently adhering to this program, despite its challenges. If you thoroughly contemplate and devote yourself, the eventual rewards will certainly be worthwhile.

E-Cigarettes, commonly referred to as Electronic Cigarettes and also known as nicotine delivery systems.

Electronic cigarettes are battery-powered devices equipped with cartridges containing nicotine, flavorings, and additional substances. In juxtaposition to conventional cigarettes, the electronic cigarette solely serves as a means of nicotine delivery.

The individual engages in the inhalation of the vapor, comprising nicotine and various chemicals synthesized by the electronic cigarette. The individual consumes the vaporized amalgamation of propylene glycol and nicotine by inhaling, imitating the action of smoking a cigarette. The e-cigarette is devoid of tobacco, combustion, and any resulting smoke. A refined and scorching mist is generated.

Certain electronic cigarettes even incorporate an illuminated tip to enhance their resemblance to conventional cigarettes. Nevertheless, certain varieties bear a resemblance to ballpoint pens. Several electronic cigarettes have the capacity for repeated use.

Cartridges have the option of being refilled or replaced, and they are available in various nicotine concentrations and flavors, such as menthol, cherry, chocolate, mint, and orange. In addition, there are cartridges available in the market which purport to have no traces of nicotine, despite studies conducted by the US Food and

Drug Administration (FDA) revealing the presence of nicotine in such products.

In spite of extensive dissemination as a purportedly healthier substitute for tobacco cigarettes and a potentially beneficial aid for smoking cessation, the World Health Organization (WHO) has ascertained that there is inadequate evidence to substantiate the claims regarding the safety and effectiveness of electronic cigarettes as a nicotine replacement therapy. A recent study conducted by the Food and Drug Administration has revealed the presence of multiple hazardous compounds and well-acknowledged carcinogens in electronic cigarettes.

Hookah

Shisha, a blend of nicotine with various fruit or vegetable flavors, is commonly consumed through the use of a water-vessel device known as a hookah.

Hookahs consist of three primary components, namely the head, the body water basin, and the hose. In formal tone: "The heating of hookahs typically occurs by means of a charcoal fire, facilitating the smoking of tobacco or Shisha."

The World Health Organization cautions that the level of smoke inhaled during an average one-hour hookah session exceeds that of a solitary cigarette by 100 to 200 times. Tobacco smoke comprises substantial quantities of carbon monoxide, heavy metals, and carcinogenic substances, even following dilution by water. Consider the following alternative phrasing in a formal tone: "The usage of a hookah apparatus also results in the inhalation of substantial quantities of nicotine, the highly addictive substance found in tobacco."

The act of engaging in hookah smoking has demonstrated a correlation with a multitude of adverse health conditions, encompassing malignancies affecting the lungs, oral cavity, and various other bodily systems. Additionally, it has been associated with the manifestation of cardiovascular ailments and respiratory infections.

The consumption of tobacco through smoking carries inherent risks, as the heating process of tobacco gives rise to detrimental byproducts like carbon monoxide, heavy metals, and carcinogenic chemicals. Herpes, tuberculosis, and hepatitis are among the various oral and respiratory conditions that have been associated with the act of sharing a Hookah mouthpiece. The utilization of tobacco in any form, including hookahs, presents identical health hazards.

Kreteks

Clove cigarettes are commonly referred to as Kreteks (pronounced "cree-techs"). Kreteks, imported from Indonesia, typically contain ingredients such as tobacco, cloves, and various additives. Scientifically conducted machine smoking studies have demonstrated that kreteks, similar to bidis, possess notably higher levels of nicotine, carbon monoxide, as well as soot compared to conventional cigarettes.

Kretek smokers, particularly individuals with preexisting conditions such as asthma or respiratory issues, have a higher propensity to experience acute lung damage. Based on the current body of research, it has been observed that individuals who regularly smoke kretek are considerably more prone to experiencing a decline in pulmonary function, with a likelihood ranging from

13 to 20 times higher in comparison to those who do not partake in smoking.

Unlike conventional cigarettes, there is no evidence to suggest that kreteks are any less detrimental.

Pipe

The three primary constituents of a pipe include the bowl, the stem, and the mouthpiece. Tobacco is inserted into the pipe and ignited. Subsequently, the smoker proceeds to intake the smoke through the stem and mouthpiece of the pipe.

Pipe smoking has been associated with malignancies of the oral cavity, buccal mucosa, lingual region, pharynx, lungs, pancreas, kidneys, bladder, colon, and cervix, alongside chronic obstructive pulmonary disease, stroke, and coronary heart disease. An additional consequence of pipe smoking is the occurrence of a hairy tongue, characterized by the formation of small fuzzy protuberances on the tongue. The tobacco has the potential to cause staining on the lumps, resulting in the tongue acquiring a discolored or potentially blackened appearance.

Smokeless Tobacco, Alternatively Referred to as Chewing Tobacco

In the United States, snuff and chewing tobacco stand as the predominant alternatives to cigarettes. Loose leaf, plug, and twist are all classifications of chewing tobacco. Snuff can be obtained in various forms such as sachets, tins, or packets containing finely ground tobacco, similar to tea bag-like pouches.

While it is true that there exists a small minority of individuals who inhale snuff through the nasal passage, the predominant practice among smokeless tobacco users is to insert the substance into the buccal cavity or the interstitial space between the gingiva and the cheek. Smokeless tobacco, frequently referred to as spit tobacco or spitting tobacco, is orally consumed in a manner similar to regular tobacco, but subsequently expelled following utilization. A considerable amount of the nicotine contained within this cigarette is taken in through the oral mucosa.

The consumption of smokeless tobacco carries significant health hazards; therefore, it is imperative to refrain from using it as a substitution for cigarettes. Smokeless tobacco contains a minimum of 28 carcinogenic substances. Tobacco use has been associated with the development of gum recession, leucoplakia (a condition characterized by the presence of white patches or plaques in the oral cavity that cannot be removed by scraping), and oral cancer. Tobacco smoke inhalation does not present a viable health-conscious substitute for conventional cigarettes, as it carries the inherent risk of fostering addictive behaviors and dependencies.

What Is The Optimal Approach To Cessation Of Smoking?

Prior to delving into the sequential outline of the book, let us pause momentarily to discuss the prevailing methods frequently employed by individuals in their endeavor to cease smoking. Frankly speaking, every approach has its own merits and drawbacks, which is why we have integrated multiple strategies into our habit framework.

Allow us to examine five notable strategies for quitting smoking:" "Let us now assess five predominant methods for ceasing smoking:" "Please allow this review to expound upon five prevalent approaches to quitting smoking:

#1: Abstaining abruptly and relying solely on one's determination.

You cease smoking abruptly. You discard any remaining cigarettes and make a conscious decision, henceforth, to abstain from smoking. The precise delineation of when you choose to terminate your engagement is evident.

Pros:

you can start immediately

no slow weaning-off period

established date of smoking cessation

You have the option to commence it today.

it doesn't cost anything

Cons:

battle with bodily and emotional dependency endure physical and mental addiction confront physiological and psychological dependency

A single mistake involving a cigarette has the potential to render this method ineffective.

very brittle

When an error is made utilizing this approach, self-accountability is attributed, thereby potentially impeding future attempts.

Option #2: Utilizing nicotine aids such as chewing gum, transdermal patches, or comparable apparatus.

This method adopts a more gradual approach, affording ample time to address and manage the cravings. Initially, one substitutes conventional cigarettes with a nicotine-containing alternative, gradually reducing nicotine intake by means of progressively diminishing doses.

Pros:

facilitates the management of both the physiological and psychological dependencies distinctly

Gradually helps you overcome your physical dependency on nicotine.

Divorces the physiological dependency from the act of tobacco consumption

meticulously crafted to maximize efficacy through scientific design

Cons:

can be quite expensive

Even upon cessation of smoking, one remains ensnared by the lingering allure of nicotine addiction.

#3: Harnessing the strength of a robust support system.

Consider actively engaging in a support group or seeking the company of individuals who have also chosen to abstain from the habit in order to effectively maintain your commitment. Analogous to the impacts experienced when participating in Alcoholics Anonymous.

Pros:

Individuals who are present to support you

Do not experience a sense of solitude.

Resignation is regarded as a procedural matter.

By relieving the burden from your shoulders and reducing the likelihood of self-reproach

Cons:

Your support network may not always be present by your side.

If a member of your support networks commits an error, they have the potential to negatively impact you as well.

One becomes dependent on an external source of reassurance

One may discontinue without establishing the necessary psychological framework, thereby increasing the risk of relapse.

#4: Administering a prescribed pharmaceutical drug.

There exist highly potent medications, such as Chantix, that incorporate the active compound varenicline. It functions through the modulation of the neural region associated with the pleasurable response to nicotine, thereby inhibiting nicotine attachment to the corresponding receptors.

Pros:

It is capable of rapidly halting the addictive behavior.

effectively and specifically engages the addiction centers

yields prompt and efficient outcomes

necessitates the participation of a physician

Adhere to an individualized strategy designed to address your prevailing tobacco dependence.

Most effective approach to attain personal freedom

Cons:

expensive

substitutes one form of substance dependence for another

Adverse effects that may result in additional health complications.

#5. Using a vaping device.

Electronic cigarettes utilize a heating mechanism to elevate the temperature of a liquid substance, which may or may not encompass nicotine, thereby producing a vapor rather than conventional smoke (one could draw an analogy to the steam that arises from water boiling).

Pros:

You are permitted to engage in vaping within numerous locations that have smoking restrictions in place.

Enables the preservation of the physical habit while mitigating the addictive aspect.

Highly expedient and efficient method

enables gradual withdrawal from the most hazardous substances present in cigarettes

Cons:

can be unbelievably expensive

A significant number of companies are currently being acquired and absorbed by established tobacco corporations, thereby resulting in your expenditure benefiting the very same company that initially engaged in harmful practices."

You are substituting one form of tobacco consumption with another, resulting in the continuation of a habit that, at most, maintains a neutral impact.

You are dependent upon technology, and should technology fail, your entire foundation can falter. In the event that your vaping battery becomes depleted and necessitates an immediate replacement, the prospect of resorting to the purchase of exorbitantly priced vaping batteries may inadvertently lead one to relapse into the procurement of conventional cigarettes.

Prior to proceeding, I would like to allocate a distinct segment to thoroughly emphasizing the prospective hazards associated with vaping. Given the novelty of this practice, the enduring consequences of vaping remain largely indeterminate. It is possible that vaping could have equivalent or potentially more detrimental health effects compared to smoking. As a result, I include vaping as a short-term alternative to smoking, but I am not inclined to endorse its prolonged use.

The Food and Drug Administration (FDA) has implemented substantial measures to safeguard the well-being of the American population from the adverse effects of tobacco by means of novel regulations, which also encompass e-cigarettes in their scope. Vaping is widely acknowledged as possessing addictive properties, and its use is strictly prohibited for individuals under the age of eighteen.

Several adverse effects have been documented in relation to vaping, including:

Dry mouth

Sore mouth

Dizziness

Cough

Dry skin

Itchiness

Dry eyes

Nosebleeds

Bleeding gums

Headache

Tongue inflammation

Black tongue

Sleepiness

Sleeplessness

Allergies

Chest pain

Breathing problems

Despite its name, "vaping," it is important to note that the majority of the substance inhaled comprises more than just water vapor. Primarily, the substance present is propylene glycol, and prior studies have indicated its potential to induce irritation in the eyes and respiratory system. In its product safety assessment for propylene glycol, the Dow Chemical Company recommends individuals avoid inhaling the chemical.

A recent investigation conducted by Goniewicz and fellow researchers, published in Nicotine & Tobacco Research, has unearthed that e-liquids, when subjected to elevated temperatures, have the potential to generate carbonyls that could be harmful. Furthermore, these findings demonstrate that levels of the carcinogenic substance formaldehyde, typically found in tobacco smoke, were detected in similar quantities. Finally, it should be noted that certain additives present in e-cigarettes have the potential to be harmful.

Developing a Suitable Strategy for Your Needs

The majority of cessation programs, approaches, techniques, and methodologies are centered on the concept of eradicating the smoking behavior. The primary rationale for the widespread popularity of vaping at present, and the method that most individuals perceive as optimal and efficacious, pertains to its utilization of a replacement ideology which substitutes detrimental habits with superior alternatives.

If none of the aforementioned approaches appear to align with your needs, do not hesitate to explore alternative and unconventional strategies. Conduct thorough research, seek insights from individuals who have successfully ceased their habit, engage in a relevant Facebook community, such as ours, and inquire about the strategies being employed by fellow members. Certain individuals achieved success through alternative methods, including hypnosis, self affirmation, Pilates, or even laser therapy. Nonetheless, their ability to successfully cease their addiction remains the paramount consideration.

One of our esteemed readers expressed that he had exhaustively attempted various approaches, yet none proved successful. He exhibited profound desperation, ultimately opting to enroll in a program provided by the Seventh-day Adventist Church, despite lacking formal affiliation with the organization. Following a five-day series of seminars, during which various techniques were demonstrated, including the cold mitten friction technique, employing a support partner, and altering one's habitual seating position, among other strategies, he made the decision to quit smoking and has remained smoke-free ever since.

Moving forward, our primary objective will be to employ the most effective strategies tailored to your needs, as a component of an overarching strategy aimed at cultivating a wholesome way of life, gradually incorporating small and manageable habits.

Upon considering the advantages and disadvantages of the aforementioned common alternatives, you may find yourself inclined to utilize certain options while disregarding others. Our objective is to reach a state wherein you are no longer dependent on any of these practices - be it chewing gum, e-cigarettes, or nicotine patches - to serve as a barrier between you and your addiction. Consequently, we intend to entirely supplant that habit. You shall embark upon the trajectory of triumph, wherein the inclination to engage in smoking shall dissipate. We intend to address the underlying source of temptation, alleviating the need for you to endure any arduous challenges throughout this process. Instead, you will discover that it remarkably facilitates both your emotional well-being and the implementation aspects.

Please examine this list and determine which approaches you find agreeable and which ones you do not. Research conducted by the Centers for Disease Control and Prevention (CDC) has indicated that the integration of various methodologies is the optimal strategy for achieving maximum efficacy. The synergy of determination, empathetic encouragement, and the guidance of a healthcare practitioner can constitute a powerful recipe for achievement when one finds themselves entrenched in the journey of addiction.

There is no universally applicable, flawless solution. Alternatively, we will provide you with a structured framework that can be customized to align with your individual circumstances.

Reflection Questions

May I inquire about the methods you have previously attempted but did not succeed with?

What is the primary obstacle you face in discontinuing this habit/activity?

What is your greatest apprehension regarding the process of discontinuing?

Upon considering each of these methods, what would you identify as the most prominent drawback?

Why do these methodologies prove ineffective for a significant proportion of individuals whilst yielding favorable outcomes for a limited few?

Your Action Plan

As we transition into the subsequent phase of this literary work, our primary emphasis shall be directed towards execution, for the responsibility now lies upon you. To initiate the process, we shall engage in a collaborative effort.

It is referred to as the "one-day resignation."

In essence, you will abstain from smoking abruptly, without any gradual reduction, for a duration of twenty-four hours.

This implies that upon awakening tomorrow morning, you will refrain from smoking until you have completed another sleep cycle. You will be undergoing a complete twenty-four-hour cessation period of smoking, after which we will meticulously examine each phase of the procedure. Throughout your journey, you will document your complete experience in a journal.

Certain individuals have a pronounced inclination to indulge in a cigarette as their initial act upon waking up. Furthermore, some individuals require it promptly following a meal, in the occurrence of a stressful event, or during their morning commute. We aim to compile a comprehensive inventory and formulate a meticulous strategy centered on your habitual patterns, in order to discern every factor that triggers your smoking behavior. We shall refer to this list subsequently to further tailor our habit stacking plan with the intent of substituting your smoking habit.

Please note that this constitutes merely the initial phase of the procedure and not the entirety of it.

In the event that you make an unintended mistake and indulge in smoking during lunchtime, endeavor to abstain from further cigarette consumption for the remainder of the day. Please assess and evaluate the intensity of your cravings or triggers individually, assigning a numerical rating on a scale of one to ten for each occurrence. If one were to make an error and indulge in a cigarette, it would undoubtedly be deemed a considerable transgression. The intensity of the longing was so great that it surpassed your capacity for self-control. That's OK. Our primary focus will be on identifying and isolating the most potent triggers, and prioritizing their mitigation as we progress through this undertaking.

Dedicate ample time to the art of journaling and developing a deep understanding of oneself. By abstaining from smoking for a day, you will discern stimuli that were previously imperceptible. After the completion of this process, kindly proceed to join me in the subsequent chapter.

The Effects Of Smoking

The act of smoking cigarettes entails a multitude of effects on the human body. Certainly, there may be favorable outcomes to consider; however, the notable disadvantages are substantial enough to give one pause in opting for an alternate choice. Presented below are several adverse repercussions associated with the habit of smoking. While it is possible that you are already familiar with the majority of these ideas, it remains worthwhile to underscore them regardless.

Respiratory ailments - The inhalation of cigarette smoke exerts a profound impact on pulmonary function. With each inhalation of smoke, numerous chemical compounds are introduced into your system, posing potential harm to various components of the respiratory tract. The inhalation of smoke leads to the entrapment of toxins within pulmonary tissues, resulting in the manifestation of symptoms such as cough, common cold, influenza, and various infections. Furthermore, it gives rise to various pulmonary ailments, such as emphysema (characterized by the deterioration of lung alveoli), bronchitis (the inflammation of the bronchial tubes), and chronic obstructive pulmonary disease (COPD). Moreover, smokers are also found to have an elevated susceptibility to various types of lung cancer.

Cardiovascular issues - Smoking exerts a comprehensive impact on the circulatory system. The primary active ingredient found in cigarettes, nicotine, induces vasoconstriction. Peripheral artery disease is associated with persistent pathological vasoconstriction. Additionally, smoking has been found to elevate blood pressure levels, thereby heightening an individual's susceptibility to cardiovascular ailments such as heart disease and strokes. Furthermore, smoking magnifies the susceptibility to atherosclerosis through the reduction of HDL levels and the promotion of cholesterol accumulation within the arterial walls. Finally, it is important to note that individuals who smoke have an elevated susceptibility to the development of leukemia when compared to those who do not engage in smoking.

Complications in the gastrointestinal system - Prolonged tobacco use leads to degradation of oral wellbeing. Smoking tobacco has the potential to give rise to oral health issues, including but not limited to gingivitis, periodontitis, dental decay, and halitosis. Furthermore, the act of cigarette smoking induces a decline in appetite, thereby increasing the risk of malnourishment and digestive disturbances related to excessive stomach acid secretion. Furthermore, smoking is also known to elicit the formation of malignancies within the gastrointestinal system, particularly in the oral cavity, pharynx, esophagus, and gastric region.

Adverse Impacts on the Reproductive System - Cigarette smoking detrimentally affects the capacity to engage in successful reproduction. As a result of diminished blood circulation to the peripheral regions, it also undermines sexual function. One explicit instance of a consequence stemming from diminished circulation of blood is the development of erectile dysfunction. Furthermore, smoking greatly diminishes the probability of attaining orgasm in males and females. Pregnant women who engage in the habit of smoking face an elevated likelihood of experiencing complications, such as placental abnormalities, preterm birth, or spontaneous termination of their pregnancy. Offspring born to smoking mothers commonly exhibit significantly reduced birth weight and may manifest developmental abnormalities.

Neurological complications - The act of smoking cigarettes also has an impact on the nervous system. Nicotine, being a CNS stimulant, elicits a transient surge in vitality. Nevertheless, once the effects subside, individuals begin to experience a profound sense of fatigue, thereby instilling a desire to resume smoking. This particular pattern has the potential to foster habitual behaviors. Over an extended duration, it has the potential to result in diminished olfactory and gustatory capabilities. In addition, it gives rise to ocular impairments, encompassing ailments like macular degeneration and cataracts. The cessation of smoking may give rise to certain cognitive impairments, including but not limited to anxiety, depression, and irritability.

Prolonged cigarette smoking is accompanied by additional health complications, leading to systemic consequences that impact the entirety of the human body. Furthermore, aside from the detrimental impact on the smoker's well-being, individuals who are subjected to secondhand smoke are also susceptible to the onset of various ailments. Various sectors, including governmental institutions and the medical field, are advocating for measures to regulate the proliferation of cigarette smoking.

1

Cease the act of smoking through the use of hypnosis and self-hypnotherapy.

H

ypnotherapy

today is

Now recognized for its efficacy in treating certain health conditions such as smoking cessation. Cessation of tobacco use can be challenging, but the use of analgesics can be useful in assisting individuals in managing this type of health issue. You can find additional information regarding cessation of smoking through the practice of hypnosis at this location.

In contemporary times, hypnotherapy has gained recognition for its efficacy in addressing certain health conditions, such as aiding in smoking cessation. Deterring smoking cessation can be challenging, but analgesics can provide assistance in addressing this particular health issue. Valuable information regarding the use of hypnosis to quit smoking can be found here.

There exists a more optimal and precise approach to halt smoking, which is a self-hypnosis smoking cessation program. It is a fact that analgesics have been proven to be the most effective method for smoking cessation. It can be confidently affirmed that it is not 100% accurate.

However, this approach proves to be the most effective method for cessation, not only from a statistical standpoint, but also in terms of its efficacy in preventing relapse through the utilization of hypnosis. Moreover, self-administered cessation programs for individuals with overconfidence and the desire to quit smoking can be undertaken within the confines of one's household, obviating the necessity of external travel arrangements and financial expenses. Based on statistics, there is a high likelihood that you will quit smoking by utilizing hypnosis, which is regarded as a safe natural method. This approach is effective, as it lacks any adverse effects or emotional distress and minimizes the associated risks, all while being cost-effective when compared to the expenses incurred from smoking.

Why is this confident pain-relieving product that helps smokers quit not more widely utilized? What are your expectations in terms of the implications when engaging in the practice of smoking cessation? It appears that the aforementioned agency exhibits deficiencies in grammar, as English does not seem to be their strong suit, or they engage in hasty typing, leading to omissions of certain words. Alternatively, it could imply that they possess knowledge of search engine functioning, as well as the observation that our tendency towards laziness is a consequence of such awareness. Unintentionally, albeit incidents of this nature do occur.

Indeed, consider this matter carefully, abstain from smoking? The venue dedicated to discussing methods of quitting smoking is quite spacious and provides a wide range of options. The predicament lies in determining whom or what one ought to select. In the realm of annihilation, myriad choices exist alongside numerous individuals or products considered as the "finest," yet we consistently realize the lack of veracity in promotional claims.

Regarding the utilization of purported transformative therapeutic hypnotic approaches, it is notable that their popularity is continuously on the rise, a development that fails to astonish me. People's physical well-being has deteriorated and they have grown weary of feeling unwell and fatigued. They are now seeking a resolution to their problems and recognize that simply treating the symptoms is not the solution. When it comes to confident restoration, an acronym known as TFAR can be employed.

This acronym represents a compilation of Thoughts, Emotions, Achievements, and Outcomes. You may observe that each expectation that we acknowledge eventually culminates in the sentiments we experience, which in turn influence the actions we undertake. We collectively acknowledge the presence of arduous periods, trials, and difficulties, and one viable approach to addressing them is through the utilization of assertive hypnotherapy techniques.

Alternative Approaches to Cessation of Smoking

Include the chapter's content in this section...In addition to medical interventions, as elucidated within this chapter, alternative approaches exist that can be depended upon to achieve a successful and comprehensive cessation of the habit.

Hypnosis is among the most favored alternatives that one can engage in. Numerous individuals affirm the positive outcomes it can yield for aspiring individuals wishing to quit. To be completely honest, this diverges significantly from the conjurers commonly linked to sorcery. Hypnosis is effectively inducing a profound state of relaxation. When an individual is in a state of relaxation, it becomes more feasible to effectively address the challenges they encounter, which encompasses the act of smoking. It has the potential to enhance your motivation to cease smoking and heighten your aversion toward cigarette consumption.

Throughout numerous centuries, acupuncture has been employed as a venerable therapeutic method. It is widely acknowledged as possessing the capacity to stimulate the release of endogenous pain-alleviating agents known as endorphins within our physiological system. This can facilitate a heightened state of relaxation. Furthermore, it aids in the expulsion of toxins commonly linked to the symptoms experienced during withdrawal.

Behavioral therapy is a more effective approach in resolving the issues associated with cigarette addiction. The behaviors that have been developed as a result of smoking can be more effectively modified through therapeutic interventions led by professionals. Behavioral therapy is effective in teaching individuals the skills necessary to manage and employ strategies for overcoming negative habits.

Therapies that are associated with motivation are typically offered by professionals, although they can also be accessed through online platforms and self-help literature. These therapeutic interventions serve as motivational tools to help individuals persevere, particularly during periods of hardship or emotional decline. The implementation of motivational strategies can facilitate the reinforcement of one's resolve to cease.

There exist numerous alternative options that you can access. However, an additional option is to occupy oneself with tasks or activities. Consider matters that hold greater significance than the act of smoking. Ultimately, you will experience a sense of pride in your unwavering resilience against the allure of smoking.

The Negative Ramifications Of Smoking

When Alex initiated the practice of smoking, his family expressed their disapproval, as he was fully aware of their anticipated reaction. His mother inquired about his welfare, clearly, but her curiosity dominated the conversation, desiring an explanation for his initiation. Although his loft mate had persuaded him to give it a try, Alex chose to keep his explanation succinct and straightforward. When asked by his mother, he simply stated, "I thoroughly enjoy it." It facilitates a state of relaxation for me.

Allow us to resolve any misunderstandings

Alex possessed a comprehensive understanding of the perils associated with smoking. In what way could he not be aware? From an early age, he had been instilled with the prevailing truths by his parents. The cautionary messages are clearly visible on every packet of cigarettes and in every magazine advertisement. The taste of his initial cigarette proved to be so repulsive that it made him feel nauseated. Subsequently, he made the determination to engage in smoking. Why? What is the rationale behind one's decision to choose that course of action?

Examine the underlying reasoning behind individuals' initiation of smoking. If you are a smoker, may I inquire about the factors that influenced your decision to initiate smoking?

Reasons for individuals commencing tobacco use:

• Approval: When your companions or colleagues engage in smoking and encourage your participation, it may seem advantageous to comply. It is essential for one to receive recognition, and engaging in customary behavior often assists in maintaining connections. Individuals who smoke tend to cultivate robust social connections, often congregating in designated smoking areas within workplace, educational, or public settings, or stepping away from larger gatherings to partake in smoking together.

• Perception: How do you desire others to perceive you? Smoking projects a particular image for certain individuals. The aspiration to appear trendy, unconventional, daring, or attractive may result in the choice to adopt the inclination.

• Inquisitiveness: It is possible that you were contemplating the taste or sensation associated with smoking a cigarette.

- Parents: If you were exposed to your parents' smoking habits during your upbringing, you are twice as likely to adopt smoking by the age of 21, as stated by the online publication, Clinical News Today. Typically, children tend to emulate their parents' actions more frequently than they heed their words.

- Media influence: The continued impact of the favorable portrayal of smoking in films, television, and online platforms continues to shape the minds of young individuals. While much of it may operate on a subliminal level, the behaviors exhibited by entertainers, sports personalities, and prominent individuals often carry as much influence as parental role models. According to the findings of the Public Foundations of Wellbeing, individuals in their youth who exhibit a significant inclination towards the depiction of smoking in movies are found to be more than three times as likely to experiment with smoking or develop a smoking habit, compared to those who have minimal exposure.

•Weight management: Some individuals initiate or resume smoking as a means to regulate their body weight. According to a scholarly article published in the American Diary of Clinical Nourishment, it is elucidated that the nicotine present in cigarettes induces higher energy expenditure within the body, thereby resulting in an elevated metabolic rate. Moreover, as widely acknowledged, it potentially reduces your appetite. In accordance with this perspective, it can be observed that individuals who smoke generally tend to have a lower body weight. It is highly probable that you have encountered former smokers expressing discontent over their weight gain subsequent to quitting smoking.

- Stress relief aid: A college student confessed that she resorted to smoking in order to alleviate feelings of tension. Her academic performance was declining, and she was beginning to experience the mounting pressures of the end of the semester. Notwithstanding her trepidation regarding its potential impact on her performance in the track team, she made the decision to give it a try.

In any case, may I inquire as to the rationale behind your decision? Regardless of when you have commenced, your justifications hold no significance. The raw reality is that deep down, it is quite possible that you are cognizant of the fact that smoking should be avoided. Upon closer examination, it becomes apparent that smoking does not fare favorably in terms of its negative effects.

CHAPTER 1

THE DECISION

I kindly request that you disregard any information you may have come across, whether through hearing, reading, or being informed, regarding the perceived challenges associated with quitting smoking. I kindly request you to embrace a mindset of openness, reset your perspectives, and ready yourself for a fresh start; any preceding events hold no significance, thus it is best to leave them in the past. It marks the dawning of a fresh day. Disregard all previous failed endeavors and futile attempts to quit smoking, for they were unsuccessful solely due to the absence of an appropriate solution. I shall provide you with the aforementioned solution.

Our shortcomings have the potential to become our most potent asset. Frequently, they lead us to a critical juncture. Look at it this way, it's your past attempts to stop smoking that brought you here today. Your previous endeavors to discontinue smoking have equipped you for this particular juncture. I must acknowledge that while we may not have a personal acquaintance, I possess an understanding of the emotions you are experiencing. I am cognizant of the difficulties, the vexations, the uncertainties, and the apprehensions that you experience. I am acquainted with you, as I have previously occupied a position similar to yours. I was previously completely subservient to cigarettes, and I detested every moment of it.

In contrast to prevailing beliefs or societal notions, it should be acknowledged that quitting does not necessarily have to be arduous or unattainable. That's one of the biggest lies ever perpetrated on the American public. Each day does not have to be a arduous endeavor, where one must consistently battle the inclination to smoke upon awakening. If such a circumstance were to arise, one might ponder why individuals would ever choose to cease. Pray, who would willingly choose to lead a life of such nature? Neither me, nor you, nor anyone else!

Tobacco consumption represents the foremost avoidable factor contributing to illness, impairment, and mortality within the United States.

Annually, approximately 443,000 individuals succumb prematurely to the detrimental effects of smoking or exposure to secondhand smoke, while an additional 8.6 million individuals endure the burden of severe ailments directly caused by smoking. Notwithstanding these risks, an estimated 46.6 million adults in the United States engage in cigarette smoking.

Nevertheless, the adverse repercussions of smoking extend beyond the individual who engages in the habit. Approximately 88 million individuals residing in the United States, who do not engage in smoking themselves, are subjected to the inhalation of secondhand smoke, with children aged 3-11 years comprising 54% of this vulnerable population. Even a brief duration of exposure can pose significant risks, as nonsmokers are exposed to a multitude of toxins present in cigarette smoke that are comparable to those inhaled by active smokers.

Exposure to secondhand smoke has been found to contribute to the development of severe illnesses and fatalities, such as heart disease and lung cancer in individuals who do not smoke. Moreover, children exposed to secondhand smoke are at an increased risk of experiencing adverse health effects, including sudden infant death syndrome, acute respiratory infections, ear complications, and heightened frequency and severity of asthma attacks. Annually, an approximate count of 3,000 non-smoking individuals in the United States succumb to lung cancer, primarily attributed to the inhalation of secondhand smoke.

What's in a Cigarette?

Cigarettes contain an estimated total of 600 ingredients. Upon combustion, these substances give rise to an excess of 4,000 chemical compounds. A minimum of 50 of these chemicals have been identified as carcinogens, with a significant proportion demonstrating toxic properties.

Numerous chemicals of similar nature can also be detected in commonly used consumer products, albeit accompanied by cautionary labels. Despite the fact that the public is being cautioned about the hazardous nature of the poisons present in these products, a similar advisory regarding the toxins contained in tobacco smoke is conspicuously absent.

Presented below are a selection of the constituents found in tobacco smoke, along with their alternative sources:

Acetone, present in nail polish remover

Acetic Acid - a constituent used in hair coloring products

Ammonia, a prevalent cleaning agent used in households

Arsenic, an element commonly found in rat poison

Benzene can be encountered in rubber cement.

Butane is employed in the composition of lighter fluid.

Cadmium is the principal constituent in the acid used in batteries.

Carbon Monoxide is emitted in automobile exhaust gases.

Formaldehyde – embalming fluid

Hexamine is a compound that is commonly found in the lighter fluid used for barbecuing.

Lead - utilized in electrical storage devices.

Napthalene is a component found in mothballs.

Methanol is a primary constituent in the composition of rocket propellants.

Nicotine is employed as an insecticide.

Tar is a substance utilized for the purpose of constructing and surfacing roadways.

Toluene is employed in the production of paint, resulting in the deaths of over 46,000 individuals due to heart disease annually. Additionally, a considerable number of children, ranging from 150,000 to 300,000 under the age of 18 months, experience lower respiratory tract infections.

In addition to this extensive health impact, there exists a substantial financial burden attributable to tobacco consumption, exceeding $96 billion annually in healthcare expenses and an additional $97 billion annually in productivity losses.

Did you know?

Fifty percent of smokers will ultimately succumb to smoking-related mortality. Indeed, that is correct, a 50% success rate.

Tobacco is the sole consumer product that, when used as intended, is responsible for the demise of half its users.

Fifty percent of individuals who engage in long-term smoking and fail to quit this habit will experience premature death as a direct result of smoking-related ailments. Individuals who engage in smoking possess a two-fold higher probability of mortality during their middle-aged years, compared to those who do not partake in the habit.

Children imitate the behavior they witness.

Certain parents fail to fully comprehend the extent of their authority in shaping their children's choices pertaining to smoking. The smoking habits and attitudes towards smoking displayed by parents play a crucial role in determining the likelihood of children and adolescents initiating and persisting with smoking. According to research findings, students who were raised by at least one parent who indulged in smoking were found to have a tripled likelihood of becoming daily smokers, in comparison to those whose parents did not engage in smoking. If it is considered acceptable by our parents, then it is deemed acceptable for me as well.

Smoking deprives your loved ones of a span of 15 years from your life.

Research suggests that individuals who succumb to a disease caused by smoking experience, on average, a reduction in life expectancy of approximately 15 years.

All cigarettes are deadly

There is a widespread belief among individuals that the usage of tobacco labeled as 'light' or 'mild' carries lesser health risks in comparison to the consumption of regular tobacco. Nevertheless, smoking "light" or "mild" cigarettes does not entail a lesser degree of safety. The levels of tar and nicotine found in 'light' cigarettes are equivalent to those in regular cigarettes, and it is possible that 'light' cigarettes could result in higher intake of carbon monoxide in comparison to regular cigarettes.

Chapter 2 - Seek Professional Assistance and Initiate the Cessation Journey

You need both mental and physical help to quit smoking. It is indeed fortunate that there exists a multitude of options available to seek assistance for mental well-being.

Let us commence a dialogue on the subject of mental assistance.

Online and telephonic assistance for smoking cessation: The utilization of online and telephonic services has proven to be highly beneficial. These services are accessible during evening hours and over the weekends. They do not entail any form of driving, babysitting, or transportation. These services can be seamlessly integrated into your hectic schedule, ensuring no time is wasted. According to experts, individuals who availed themselves of telephone and web-based services exhibited a success rate that was twice as high as individuals who did not utilize these services for assistance. Additionally, these services will prove beneficial if you have reservations regarding personal counseling.

Enroll in cessation support programs and engage with smoking cessation groups: Ceasing the habit of smoking can pose formidable challenges, particularly when attempted in isolation. Enroll in programs and participate in support groups dedicated to assisting individuals in their journey to cease smoking. Through the utilization of various programs and support groups, you will gain access to opportunities for effective communication with individuals who have triumphantly conquered their nicotine addiction. Engage in dialogue with individuals who have accomplished remarkable achievements, draw inspiration from their stories of triumph, and implement empirically validated strategies to achieve success in your endeavor to cease tobacco consumption. It is to be understood that you are not solitary in this endeavor. Individuals have emerged victorious, and thus, you too possess the capability to triumph. Hospitals, health departments, community centers, national organizations, and work sites provide smoking cessation programs.

When choosing a cessation aid, there are several key factors that you need to be aware of. You are encountering a formidable challenge, and it is imperative for you to obtain a comprehensive support program that will genuinely assist you. Ensure that the programs you seek comprise a minimum of four weekly sessions, each spanning a duration of 20 to 30 minutes. Consider participating in support initiatives that provide extensive sessions and are facilitated by competent and experienced group leaders. Exercise caution when encountering programs that provide brief interventions without any subsequent support, impose exorbitant charges, market questionable supplements or pills, or guarantee a rapid resolution.

Harness the power of hypnosis to successfully overcome tobacco addiction. Recent research findings indicate that hypnosis has demonstrated favorable outcomes among individuals with a habitual smoking pattern. Hypnosis should not be misconstrued as a stereotypical method depicted in movies or television. In light of the evolving times, it has come to pass that individuals of professional stature, bestowed with advanced academic credentials obtained from esteemed educational institutions, are engaging in the application of hypnosis within renowned medical establishments. Hypnosis does not come at a low cost; the rates commence at $80 per hour and can escalate up to $200 per hour. The number of sessions required to observe favorable outcomes may vary based on the extent of your circumstances, typically ranging from one to four sessions. A wide array of methodologies exists. Typically, the induction of hypnosis involves initiating a phase of tranquil respiration and vivid mental imagery, subsequently inducing a state of profound relaxation.

A hypnotherapist facilitates the induction of a focused and highly receptive state in a patient, subsequently substituting detrimental thoughts and anxieties with constructive and wholesome thoughts and perspectives in a gradual manner. According to Dr. John McGrail, a reputable practitioner of hypnotherapy, the approach involves treating the human subconscious mind as analogous to a computer hard drive. In this process, outdated programming is replaced with new and effective software. Although hypnosis is generally effective, it is important to note that it is not a universal solution. The primary determinant is the patient's determination. In order for hypnosis to be an effective method for quitting smoking, it is imperative that one is resolute in their decision to cease this habit. Select a highly esteemed hypnotherapist to achieve superior outcomes.

Endorsement from loved ones: Numerous ex-smokers attest to the vital role played by their familial and social connections, as they provide indispensable psychological reinforcement throughout the process of overcoming tobacco addiction. Individuals such as your colleagues and medical practitioner can provide assistance and motivation. Inform your acquaintances about your intention to resign and inquire for recommendations. Refrain from interacting with individuals who smoke and instead socialize with individuals who have successfully quit smoking or those who have never smoked.

Daily Habits For Assisting Smoking Cessation

Let us start simple. Initiating a transformation necessitates a personal internal shift. It is unnecessary to rely on the guidance of a medical professional or a mental health specialist to provide advice on the appropriate course of action. There exist certain routine actions that one may partake in to effectively aid in the cessation of smoking. Quitting smoking can be a formidable challenge due to the deeply ingrained thoughts and habits that have become associated with this habit. Once an individual has transitioned into a heavy smoker, their psychological and behavioral patterns become interwoven with the act of smoking and the perceived relief it provides. Altering mundane and routine cigarette habits can significantly contribute to your endeavor of cessation.

Kindly commit these strategies to memory. Therefore, when you experience the inclination to engage in smoking, adopt a strategy of postponing it. Nevertheless, this persistent craving can persist for a minimum of 5 minutes, which can be incredibly unbearable for a smoker, given its intensity; making it highly likely that one would succumb to it. Rather than seeking immediate satisfaction, consider deferring such satisfaction. Please divert your attention towards alternative activities or matters. It should be an activity that you have a strong passion for or derive great pleasure from engaging in. Exercising patience is of utmost importance, given that initially, one may encounter limitations in accomplishing the task. However, with a strong determination and persistent effort on your part, you will eventually accomplish the task. As the passage of time ensues, you will observe a notable reduction in the frequency of these urges. This marks a significant stride in the direction of attaining your objective of quitting smoking.

Another point worth noting is that when individuals extend an invitation to partake in cigarette smoking, it is advisable to politely decline to the greatest extent feasible. Since you need to get your way out of smoking and fellow smokers too, it is therefore understood that you should be able to surround yourself with people who don't smoke. Enhancing your support network with individuals who possess the ability to consistently persuade and reinforce your motivations for quitting will facilitate the process of cessation. It is imperative to acknowledge that cigarettes do not serve as your closest companion, nor do they mitigate stress more effectively than engaging in social activities or partaking in enjoyable pastimes to alleviate tension.

Ceasing the habit would be equally facilitated if you ensure that your packet of cigarettes and accompanying lighter remain inaccessible. By adhering to this approach, you will gradually reduce the quantity of cigarettes consumed on a daily basis over the course of successive weeks. Not only are you capable of undertaking the endeavor to cease smoking, but you also possess the ability to eradicate conspicuous indications of smoking, such as the lingering scent of smoke on your attire, within your residence, and in your hair. When endeavoring to abstain from smoking, it is advisable to concurrently refrain from consuming coffee, carbonated beverages, tea, and alcoholic beverages. Please continue this task to the maximum extent possible, and observe substantial alterations in the forthcoming days and weeks. By abstaining from the intake of such detrimental substances, you enhance your ability to concentrate on your objectives, thereby cultivating them as sources of motivation, while concurrently mitigating adverse thoughts and impulses.

Returning to directing one's attention towards engaging in a passion, there exists a plethora of alternatives that can be substituted for the habit of smoking cigarettes. Once again, emphasizing the significance resides in devoting attention to activities that bring you pleasure, while actively distancing oneself from behaviors associated with smoking.

You have the option to substitute your engagement in cigarette smoking with engaging in physically demanding activities instead. There are numerous pursuits that warrant your attention and should serve as a means of diverting your focus. Among these include fitness training, swimming, badminton, soccer, cycling, volleyball, dancing, running, and many more! By doing this, you are also taking care of your body and making sure that you get the right amount of exercise that you should have in order to become fit.

It is highly recommended that you also seek out enjoyable activities and pursue other hobbies that genuinely bring you joy. Engaging in such endeavors will not only provide ample opportunities for laughter, but will also allow you to partake in these experiences alongside your friends and loved ones.

Whenever you find yourself with idle time, it is highly advisable to engage in activities that occupy your hands, such as playing with a rubber band, holding a pencil, or perhaps even manipulating a paper clip. If one engages in habitual smoking, they have likely developed a strong familiarity with holding a cigarette, believing that it may provide temporary relief from emotional and physical burdens. Therefore, it is highly beneficial to participate in activities that require frequent hand usage, such as drawing, engaging in do-it-yourself projects, pursuing crafts, practicing photography, or even allocating time for petting your dog. This is also a highly effective method of alleviating stress.

Evidently, in addition to keeping your hands occupied, it is imperative that you find alternative means to occupy your mouth apart from habitually having a cigarette in it on a daily basis. In the event that you experience the inclination to smoke, it is advisable to substitute this behavior by chewing gum, brushing your teeth, or even chewing on cinnamon sticks. Increasing your water intake can also be an effective strategy to address this urge.

Set up Your Plan

If one has devised a prudent strategy, it can be inferred that one has effectively conquered a substantial portion of their endeavor. There exists a renowned theory which can be employed in combatting the issue of smoking. The theory is commonly recognized as START.

There exists a comprehensive elucidation of the Strategic Techniques for Achieving Resolute Termination (START) that aligns seamlessly with the long-term objective of permanent smoking cessation. Here it is:

S signifies the requirement to establish a specific date. You must establish a definitive date at which you will cease the habit of smoking. Refrain from convincing yourself that you will cease smoking either tomorrow or in the imminent future. Arrange a designated day, which serves as the primary objective to accomplish. Once you have completed the task of organizing the day, it is imperative that you consciously reinforce the notion that this is the day on which you will cease smoking. In addition, kindly ensure that the chosen day falls within the upcoming week, as initiating the task promptly yields advantageous outcomes.

T signifies the act of formally informing individuals of one's emancipation from the habit of smoking. Articulate your plan in extensive detail to the individuals in your immediate vicinity. This holds significance as informing individuals about your decision will contribute to the cultivation of your authority.

A represents anticipation. It is imperative to affirm to oneself an unwavering commitment to not relapse into smoking, while concurrently developing meticulous strategies to prevent any future instances of smoking.

R shall serve as the symbol for the elimination of items pertaining to one's residence, automobile, and potentially all other locations. The primary catalyst for relapse into smoking is individuals' inability to resist the temptation upon encountering smoking paraphernalia once more. It is not necessarily required to be the cigarette. It could serve the purpose of being a lighter, ashtray, or any other item pertinent to one's smoking activities. Ensure that all items pertaining to smoking are discarded from your vicinity.

The concluding letter T is a representation that signifies verbal communication. If the alternative strategies prove ineffective, it would be necessary to consult with a physician in order to resolve this matter. It is important to always bear in mind that there exists a viable solution to overcome the habit of smoking. The inability to overcome smoking without assistance does not denote weakness, nor does it imply impossibility. Your physician will provide assistance by way of medications, nicotine patches, and nicotine gums.

www.ingramcontent.com/pod-product-compliance
Lightning Source LLC
Chambersburg PA
CBHW050250120526
44590CB00016B/2294